IMAGES

Around
Cranleigh

Michael Miller

In 1890, Cranleigh was a largely undeveloped rural community of some 2,000 inhabitants. The Obelisk remains its unique feature and the curious topiary clipped in the shape of a peacock is a feature of pictures of the time. In the white cottage behind was the Cranleigh Creamery which belonged to Mr Stephen Rowland, said to be the founder of modern Cranleigh. Soon after this picture was taken it was demolished to make room for a photographer's studio, and, appropriately, it was the early development of photography which provided a record for us all to enjoy today.

IMAGES OF ENGLAND

Around
Cranleigh

Michael Miller

NONSUCH

· First published 1995
This new pocket edition 2005
Images unchanged from first edition

Nonsuch Publishing Limited
The Mill, Brimscombe Port,
Stroud, Gloucestershire, GL5 2QG
www.nonsuch-publishing.com

British Library Cataloguing in Publication Data.
A catalogue record for this book is available from the British Library.

ISBN 1-84588-143-5

Typesetting and origination by Nonsuch Publishing Limited
Printed in Great Britain by Oaklands Book Services Limited

Contents

Introduction

My family moved into Cranleigh in 1968, the year of the floods. For the locals this was nothing new and, indeed, it seemed that water had often featured in the evolution of the area. These recollections of the past sparked off a personal desire to find out more and this, combined with a passion for collecting memorabilia, eventually led to the opportunity to record this glimpse into the past.

The origins of Cranleigh, or Cranley as it was earlier known, are obscure. The Roman roads of Stane Street passed through Ockley in the east and Farley Green in the north, although it is known that there were settlements in Snoxhall, Utworth, Canfold and Pollingfold before the Norman Conquest. Cranley itself is not mentioned in the Domesday Book, being part of the manor of Essira or Shere. By 1170 responsibility for the manor passed to one Richard de Tonbridge, who sanctioned the building of the church to provide a place of worship for the tradespeople and farm labourers from the scattered settlements in the area.

Another mystery surrounds the name itself. A commonly held belief is that cranes or herons were bred on Vachery Lake to provide a delicacy for the lord of the manor's table, although this is somewhat fanciful and unsupported by either reason or evidence. Despite this, the heron has become the symbol of the village and currently adorns a number of monuments, including the fountain and a large number of iron bollards in Stockland Square. Leigh or 'leagh' is a Saxon word for a clearing in a wood and it is known that the settlers from the Tillingbourne Valley were in the habit of visiting the Weald to provide fuel and grazing for animals. Others believe that 'cran' refers to the cranberries that grow on Winterfold, but hurt or whortleberry is the local name and the term cranberry did not come into use until much later. A more prosaic derivation is always possible. For example, the Old English word 'cranc' meaning a bend or twist in a track or river. The French 'cran' signifies an opening with no exit from which we derive the word cranny.

The Saxon kingdom of Essira later became known as Shere cum Vachery. Vachery is an Old French word meaning an enclosed area for the raising of cattle, and early maps show this as a prominent feature in comparison to Cranley itself. Development of the surrounding area was undoubtedly impeded by the clay soils which were almost impassable to wheeled vehicles during the wet winter months. Goods moving up from the South Coast were transferred to pack mules whilst the horses and carts awaited a return load. This build-up of horses probably accounts for the name of Horsham deriving from horse-ham.

Iron smelting in the Weald brought some prosperity to the area but declined again around 1573 when Elizabeth I declared that oak and beech were to be used in the building of ships and not burnt for charcoal. Local names such as Hammer Farm and Smithwood Common serve as reminders of this period. Glass-making kilns were also established at Sydney Wood near Alfold and Sommersbury near Ewhurst. However, the community would have remained rural with smallholdings supplementing their income with cloth-making, charcoal burning and coppicing the woodland. In addition, smuggling seems to have provided the occasional departure from an otherwise drab and meagre existence.

Records show that Oliver Cromwell visited Knowle in 1657 and his staff were billeted in the village. In return for their hospitality, the villagers were granted the right to hold a fair twice a year. A facsimile of the original charter can be seen in the china department of David Mann's shop.

The passing of various turnpike acts provided greatly improved access to the surrounding area. A road from Guildford to Newbridge in 1757 and a further extension from Alfold Crossways to Horsham in 1809 had both left Cranleigh somewhat isolated. Eventually, in 1818 assent was granted for the building of a further extension south of Bramley to Bucks Green passing through Wonersh, Cranleigh and Rudgwick, a distance of nine miles and at an estimated cost of £4,830 18s. Construction problems caused by the Weald clay were compounded by a lack of promised funds from subscribers. Toll gates were set up along the routes and evidence of these can still be seen at Shalford, Graffham, Gaston Gate, Cranleigh Common and Alfold Crossways. However, charges were set at a level beyond the reach of the farming community and, consequently, revenues never attained their expected levels.

At the beginning of the nineteenth century, thoughts were dominated by the threat of a possible blockade of the English Channel by Napoleon, and such fears gave great impetus to the building of a canal linking the South Coast ports to the Thames. The River Wey was made navigable between Guildford and Weybridge and a new cutting was made from Shalford to the Arun at New Bridge, passing through Bramley, Run Common and Loxwood. When opened in 1816, trade and industry grew with coal and roofing slates from South Wales arriving at Elmbridge Wharf and boats returning with loads of bricks and other merchandise for distribution to London and export from the South Coast.

The middle of the nineteenth century saw a great upsurge in the fortunes of the community and its subsequent growth. The break-up of the great estates provided an ideal opportunity for those with fortunes made in the colonies to develop substantial estates in a pleasant part of the country, conveniently placed for travel to London. The National School completed in 1847 replaced the dame schools and the church was extensively restored. A new rectory was built adjacent to the church and the old one was put at the disposal of the village for use as a hospital, the first of its kind in the country.

Cranleigh School opened in 1865 as 'The Surrey County School' for, as a contemporary article in *The Illustrated London News* describes, 'parents of the middle class or persons of moderate incomes'.

By far the most significant event of the time was the coming of the railway in 1865. As early as 1867 the volume of post carried by the railway brought a request from the postal authorities for a change in the spelling of the name from Cranley to

Cranleigh to avoid confusion with Crawley. At its peak in 1890, the villagers were provided with twelve services in a day, but a 2nd class fare of 1/4d to Guildford was still sufficient to deter all but the most determined or the most affluent. Goods traffic continued to grow, and, as a direct consequence, the canal, which was constantly dogged by insufficient depth of water, fell into almost inevitable disuse.

If one man could be said to be responsible for the development of the village above any others it would be Stephen Rowland. Stephen's uncle, Henry, purchased the large house next to Cranley House in 1835 where young Stephen grew up and eventually took over himself in 1857. He later purchased Ivy Hall Farm and, after adding a new frontage, Rowlands Stores was able to offer a range of household essentials as well as provide the village Post Office in adjacent premises. From these modest beginnings, Rowland became a major investor and benefactor. He formed the Gas Company in 1876 and was instrumental in bringing the public water supply from Hascombe in 1886. Later, in 1894, he developed a large part of the New Park estate by bridging the stream to create New Park, Avenue, Mead, Mount and Bridge roads.

In 1885, Sir Henry Peek built the Lady Peek Institute in memory of his wife, to provide a centre of recreation for the men of the village. Two years later the firm of David Mann's was established on its present site, where it has occupied a central position in village life for over one hundred years.

Also at this time, Ivy Hall Barn, which stood close to where Lloyd's Bank is now situated, was demolished, and with it the last symbol of the village's agricultural origins.

By the end of the century, the population had doubled and the need for a further church near the Common was satisfied by the opening in 1900 of St Andrew's church, subsequently demolished to provide dwellings for senior citizens.

The Village Hall, completed in 1933, has remained a central focus of social life up to the present time and the retention of the village image justifies the claim that Cranleigh is the largest village in England. Certainly old-timers can be distinguished from the newcomers by their insistence on referring to 'the village,' whereas the latter will normally speak of 'the town'.

The bulk of the material used in this book is from postcards collected by the author and this has been supplemented by photographs and other material loaned by others whose help and interest is gratefully appreciated.

Within its scope, the book looks at Cranleigh and the surrounding villages and gives an impression of a different age and another way of life. We now enjoy a greatly improved range of goods to buy, a cinema, a splendid sports centre and a whole range of leisure facilities totally unknown to the generation which is the subject of this book. Whether all the changes have been for the better, and all the improvements made in the name of progress have justified the end result, the reader is left to judge.

One

The Village

The drinking fountain and the horse trough were both donated in 1889 by Ellen Bradshaw in memory of her husband Arthur Hibbert Bradshaw, son of John Bradshaw, Lord of the Manor of Knowle. The crane surmounting the roof of the fountain is a reminder of the derivation of the name of the village, and the osier basket symbolises the ancient craft of basket-making from pliable strips of willow trees which once abounded in the district.

By far the oldest standing building, St. Nicholas Church was built in 1170 by the Norman masters of Vachery to provide a place of worship for workers on the surrounding estates. Enlarged during the 14th century and extensively restored in 1847, the south porch was added in 1864 as a memorial to Jacob Ellery. The large Cedar of Lebanon was said to have been brought back as a seed by Archdeacon Sapte from his honeymoon and planted on his return.

Above: The spacious interior owes much to the restorations of 1845 and 1862. The impressive stained glass East window, seen here, was virtually destroyed in 1944 by a flying bomb, although the replacement clear glass does give a light and airy appearance. When visiting the church look out for the curious feline head, said to be the inspiration for Lewis Carroll's Cheshire Cat.

Right: In 1880 the churchyard was extended to the main road and a wall and entrance added. Designed by Henry Woodyer, the lychgate is dedicated to the memory of John Bradshaw of Knowle. The churchyard contains a number of interesting grave markers showing the names of many of the old Cranleigh families.

Cranleigh Church, Lychgate.

The Obelisk was erected to mark the opening of the turnpike road between Rooks Hill, south of Bramley, and Bucks Green. The date of erection is not certain but is likely to be after 1818 when the road was opened. The local doctor John Ellery was the principal subscriber and arranged for the siting so that it was visible from his house, Broadoak. The mileage plates were cast in the local foundry of John Champion and the distances to Windsor and Brighton were selected for the benefit of the Prince Regent who frequently used the route on his journeys to the Brighton Pavillion. The base is constructed of local 'winklestone' and early reports have referred to the top being surmounted by a pineapple, but so far no drawings or pictures have come to light showing this particular adornment.

Village Hospital, c. 1870. When the hospital opened in 1859 it was the first of its kind in England. The old cottage was given over to the then village doctor, Dr Napper, with room for six beds. It was funded in the main by local subscription and patients paid an additional amount depending on their circumstances. It has been extended twice and when threatened with closure in the seventies funds were raised by the community to pay for the necessary modernisation.

Opened in 1847, the National School replaced several dame schools in the area. It was built from public subscription, a major contributor being Reverend Thurlow of Baynards. The two wings were added later and, at its peak, is said to have housed over two hundred pupils.

The Art Centre remained as a school until 1964 and when closed it remained empty for several years until being given to the village for use by local societies. Apart from the absence of traffic, it looks very much today as it did when this picture was taken in 1916.

Cranleighans are proud of their Village Hall and claim to be the largest village in England, despite a growing population of over 12,000. Originally intended as a war memorial, the necessary funds took a long time to materialise, despite a substantial contribution from Sir Charles Chadwyck-Healey of Wyphurst. It was finally opened in 1933 and recently benefited from a major refurbishment.

Cranleigh St. Andrew's Church

By the end of the 19th century the population at the northern end of the village had grown to such an extent that a further church had become necessary. Built to commemorate the Diamond Jubilee of Queen Victoria, St Andrew's church was dedicated in 1900 but demolished in 1975 to make room for flatlets for senior citizens.

Above: A Baptist Chapel has existed since 1828 and prospered under the Holden family and at one time included a school. The present building was opened in 1889 under the pastorage of Mr C.B. Barringer.

Right: The Wesleyan Methodist Church was erected in 1904 at a cost of £2,400 to replace an older hall outgrown by the congregation.

Cranleigh Public School opened in 1865 as the Surrey County School for children of 'middle class' families. Fees were initially set at £30 per year and the buildings were designed to take 150 pupils. From these modest beginnings the school has expanded and is now one of the largest leading public schools in the country. Four years after the opening, north and west wings were added and, later, the Chapel, which was the gift of Sir Henry Peek.

A major extension to the teaching and accommodation facilities was added in 1928–31; the architect was a Mr Cooper and the builders Higlett & Hammond of Guildford.

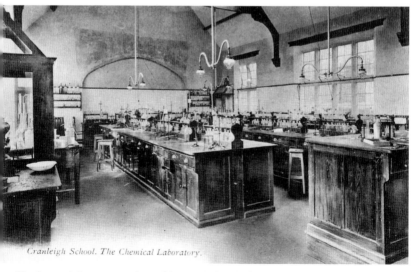

Cranleigh School. The Chemical Laboratory.

The Science Laboratory was donated by Sir Charles Chadwyck-Healey of Wyphurst and was opened in 1912. This well-equipped facility played a major part in the development of the school under the headmastership of the Rev H.A. Rhodes who remained in office until 1931.

The new 'Prep' School was built in 1913 by the local firm Warrens. A local resident recalls her father Mr Sandford setting out the foundations virtually single-handed. This picture was clearly taken before the development of the surroundings and the addition of the chapel in 1962.

Cranleigh School. The Sanatorium.

The Sanatorium was originally donated by the Right Hon. George Cubitt in 1879. Its primary purpose was to isolate TB victims and to ensure that they received ample supplies of fresh air. The shrubbery has now been removed but the building still stands as Cubitt House.

The Jubilee Fountain was erected in 1897 by the boys of Cranleigh School to commemorate the Diamond Jubilee of Queen Victoria. The gentleman in the picture is believed to be Mr George Holden and the house in the background was Windibank's grocery stores.

Above: The wonderful avenue of trees which stretches from the centre of the village to the Cricket Field was planted in 1890 through the generosity of Mr E.L. Rowcliffe of Hall Place and are of a very rare variety known as 'acer Schwerderii.' Recent reports that the trees were planted by grateful Canadians after the First World War almost certainly refer to some later in-filling but not the original planting.

Left: The War Memorial, 1921, before the inclusion of those fallen in the Second World War. Comparison with the Cenotaph in Whitehall has led to speculation that it was designed by Sir Edwin Lutyens, but so far the author has been unable to verify this.

Cranleigh War Memorial

Two

Streets and Shops

THE VILLAGE, CRANLEIGH.

The Village, 1902. The trio of shops currently housing the Camera Shop, John Alan, and the Bookshop are unusual in being aligned with their narrow gable end toward the road, presumably to reduce the costs of a wide frontage. Whilst at first sight they appear similar, they are of quite different age and build quality.

This picture shows Cromwell Cottage where Cromwell's men were stationed when he stayed at Knowle in 1657. This fine timber-framed building was annexed by David Mann's in the 1920s and now houses the china department.

Opposite above: Beadells Stores, *c.* 1880, eventually went bankrupt and the premises were purchased by David Mann and opened as a furniture store. Prior to this the village doctor is said to have lived there and part of the building was occupied by the post office. Mr Mann and his family lived behind and over the shop.

Opposite below: In the 1890s David Mann's occupied about thirty feet of frontage, the remainder being used by Arthur Parsons, the saddler. Manns later took over the whole shop and the double frontage was added in 1900. Bicycles were made, including frames and wheels, with the trade name Enterprise. In 1910 David took his two sons Samuel and Jesse into partnership but died the same year.

Above: Collins the butchers dressed for Queen Victoria's Diamond Jubilee in 1897. The shop is probably a 19th century extension but the main house can be traced back to 1690 when it was known as 'Spittle Ditch' and belonged to a family of weavers.

Left: Mr Sparkes Collins is seen here with two of his staff. Live pigs were killed in the yard at the rear of the premises and the pork can be seen hanging ready for sale.

Later the shop front was extended to give more room for groceries such as Hudson's soap and wax candles. Note the splendid pair of ornate gas lamps! Collins became noted for their celebrated pork sausages and, when the shop finally closed to make way for building development, locals were relieved to hear that sausages made to the same traditional recipe would still be available in the village.

Walter Briggs shop at London House offered a wide range of clothing, blankets, boots and shoes, later taken over by Gammons. Local residents recall a pneumatic tube system for passing money to and from the cash desk. The building has now been replaced by a modern parade, housing a bank, estate agents and a wine and spirit store.

Opposite above: The lower end of the High Street looking towards the Obelisk. Cranleigh House is behind the hedge on the right where the library now stands. The large white house was for many years an antique and furniture store belonging to Nightingales, before being demolished to make room for the extension to the Village Hospital in 1976.

Opposite below: Tanner and Chart offered a complete drapery and outfitting service and in 1911 a suit could be purchased for 25 shillings. The frontage was later extended and in more recent times was a wine bar before becoming a restaurant.

At the turn of the century the present baker's shop was a tearoom and grocer's owned by Mr Frank Winser. To the rear of this was the coal depot in which a bakehouse was built by a Mr Frederick Germany and later developed by Mr Tom Cornwall, who had previously been the landlord of The Greyhound Public House.

By 1910 Arthur Parsons, the saddlers and harness makers, had moved to new premises next to the London and Southern Counties Banks. In the centre of the picture is Stephen Rowland's Stores with the frontage added at the turn of the century. Today it houses a delicatessen and a wine and spirit merchants.

Bank Buildings, c. 1912. Shops number five and six were occupied by F.J. Delves, the hairdresser, stationer, and tobacconist. Older inhabitants recall businessmen calling in for a shave before making the train trip to London. Their personal shaving mugs were arranged on the shelves inside the shop. Many of the picture postcards used in this book were sold in the adjoining premises.

KNOWLE LANE FROM VILLAGE.

After William Hanham rebuilt Knowle House in 1823 he acquired the two plots on the corners of Knowle Lane and built two lodges in the same Italianate style as the house. This was no doubt to impress visitors and to create the false impression that his estate extended as far as the High Street.

Opposite above: In this picture the lodge on the left remains and provides premises for Mrs Boxall's Registry Office for 'Ladies and Servants'. Some time later these premises were converted to house the Co-op stores before they moved to their present modern premises.

Opposite below: The level crossing was still in use when this picture was taken, and other minor changes have taken place, although the houses remain much the same.

Knowle Lane, Cranleigh.

Knowle Lane Cranleigh.

W.H.A. 4582

The Post Office has occupied several different premises in the village. In the 1890s it was housed in the eastern portion of Ivy Hall Farm. A few years previously the large barn which stood in front was dismantled and this section of the village became accessible for development. Prior to this, the office was situated in part of David Mann's shop and the post was carried from Guildford in a cart pulled by two mastiffs.

When Stephen Rowland took over Ivy Hall Farm a new frontage was added and the property was enlarged. Rowlands Stores flourished and the Post Office expanded to cope with an ever-increasing volume of mail.

By 1911 the Post Office had moved to the corner of Knowle Lane, in premises known as Richmond House. The postmistress can be seen looking through the window and the three telegraph boys are waiting to make their deliveries. The first floor building behind, now occupied by an Italian restaurant, housed the Telephone Exchange.

The present Post Office, designed by G.A. Pearce for the Ministry of Works and opened in 1959, was built on the site of the old Greyhound Inn.

C. Hight, fruiterer and game dealer on the Common, showing stock available for Christmas. Fresh fish was delivered direct from London every day and local families were 'waited on daily'.

The top end of the High Street in 1916. Note the use of hand carts and the newspaper banner proclaiming the burning of Yarmouth pier pavilion.

This fine old seventeenth-century building on the Common housed the St Andrews bakery. From here Mr Pirie baked and delivered bread, no doubt taking advantage of freshly milled flour available from the nearby mill.

Common House Farm housed the premises of Edward Brown the butcher, poulterer and ice merchant. The shallow-sided pond provided a convenient facility for the washing of cart wheels. Despite the developments that have taken place in this area some of the old farm buildings remain to this day.

Ewhurst Road, 1913. As well as the Obelisk another famous landmark was the yew topiary tree, representing a peacock but known affectionately by the villagers as the 'Wellington boot'. The remains of this tree can still be seen in Yew Tree Cottage, which is now a vetinary surgery.

On the corner of Ewhurst and Mead roads stood Jabez Nightingale's confectionery shop and newsagents. The offerings of chocolate and ice cream obviously proved irresistible to the local children.

Looking back towards the High Street the premises on the left are occupied by Lades, the butchers. Beyond this is the White Hart public house which dates from 1867 and was taken over by George Bruford in 1883. In the distance can be seen the characteristic arched frontage of the old Village Hall.

Rye Cottage near the corner of Barhatch Lane was once a small grocery and sweet shop owned by the Ford family. Mr George Ford was trained as a carpenter but after the war he helped his wife run this little shop in Parkhouse Green. The offering of tea and cakes in the gardens earned him the nick name of 'Dicky Doughnut'.

Parkhouse Cottages in the Ewhurst Road were built in the 1920s by the local firm of Warren & Son. They were part of a ribbon development by the local authority and have recently been modernised. In the late sixties numbers 3 and 4 were demolished to provide access to the Summerlands development.

In Bedlow Lane stood Stemp's Cottage, now long since demolished. The inscription on the back of this old photograph says that twenty-one children lived here! Standing in the doorway is Charlie Cachet and the man on the right is Tom Warner.

New Park Road, 1910. The wall on the right can still be seen and the road is easily recognisable. In 1894, Stephen Rowland laid out the Woodlands Estate, which included Bridge Road, New Park Road, Woodland Avenue, Mead Road, Mount Road, The Mount and Avenue Road.

Opposite Bridge Road stands an impressive balconied house, at one time occupied by the local doctor, Dr Willis, before he moved to Horsham Road. Surgeries were held in a small outbuilding in the garden. The pair of semi-detatched houses to the left are named after places in the Lake District and were built by Holdens at the turn of the century.

Bridge Road, 1906. Development of this area was made possible by the bridging of the stream running alongside Horsham Road. Note the similarity of the houses on the right and the pair in the previous picture almost certainly built to the same plan by Holdens.

When this picture was taken Bridge Road comprised mostly open land and the substantial gabled houses in New Park Road are clearly visible. At this time, the Land Company were true to their ideal of developing the area as a whole rather than selling individual plots.

Mount Road, *c.* 1916, clearly shows Stephen Rowland's ideal of a woodland estate as evidenced in the tree planting and the paling fence running uniformly along the length of the pavement.

Properties in Mead Road are mostly semi-detached and of a similar design. Trees lining the road were already well established but a slow rate of development meant that road surfacing had to be delayed until the late twenties.

Horsham Road, 1912, looking back towards the area known as Lucks Green. The clapper bridge on the right is a prominent feature of views taken at this time, and stood for many years until being replaced. Sadly, its modern counterpart lacks the rustic charm of its predecessor.

Lucks Green, 1904. Whilst a delivery is being made a carriage passes on its way along the Horsham Road.

The corner of Mount Road and Horsham Road has changed little since this picture was taken around 1910. The road was being surfaced and the area opposite was open fields.

Three

Transport

Gaston Gate Turnpike, c. 1880. The last keeper was Mr Hubert Ketcher's grandmother, seen here by the gate. With tolls of 6d for a horse and 1/- for a pair, villagers would go a long way to avoid payment. The small toll-house has now been incorporated into a bungalow just visible behind a tall hedge.

FIB6 Cranleigh.

This peaceful scene shows how horse-drawn transport was the principal means of portage up until the First World War. Unfortunately, passage was slow and water transport offered advantage in costs and the facility of carrying considerable tonnages over large distances.

When the Wey and Arun Canal was completed in 1816 it linked the Wey Navigation at Shalford to the river Arun at Newbridge and passed through Bramley, Run Common and Loxwood. Local craftsmen together with Irish labourers and French prisoners from the Napoleonic Wars were engaged in its construction. It was never a great success and constantly suffered from a lack of water and was obviously not in use at the time of this picture.

Cranleigh Station.

Cranleigh Station, 1906. A train is just arriving from Horsham. A considerable increase in traffic was provided by the addition of a passing loop in 1880, giving commuters the choice of five trains a day to Guildford and seven to Horsham.

When the Horsham to Guildford Railway was opened in 1865, the line had five stations, Bramley, Cranley, Baynards, Rudgwick and Slinfold, and the occasion was one of great joy and celebration. In 1867 Cranley was changed to Cranleigh at the request of the postal authorities to avoid confusion with Crawley.

By 1963 the station was nearing the end of its useful life. BR 41301, a 2-6-2T class engine, is seen just about to leave for Guildford. The station buildings were demolished to make room for a modern parade of shops known as Stocklund Square. The platform levels can still be seen at the rear of the shops.

The level crossing in Knowle Lane was, at one time, operated by Mrs Cheeseman, who sat in a chair turning the big wheel which opened and shut the gates. She lived in the lodge now known as the Gate House. The old railway embankment has been preserved as the Downs Link, a popular track for walkers.

At the beginning of the century the motor car began to appear. This 1903 Regal is possibly the first petrol-driven motor vehicle to appear in the village and could be purchased at the time for the considerable sum of £130. The owner is unknown but he is accompanied by his 'motor servant' whose purpose was not to drive but to crank the starting handle and perform minor repairs during the journey. Clearly parking is not a problem when yours is the only vehicle.

For those of more modest means a motorised tricycle was a convenient means of exploring the country lanes of the Surrey hills. In this view of Pitch Hill notice the relative absence of trees compared with the present day.

Ewhurst Road, 1910, the popularity of the motor car had increased to such an extent that Frank Osbourn expanded his cycle business to include a facility for servicing and refuelling motor cars. The building is still visible and today is occupied by a fish and chip shop.

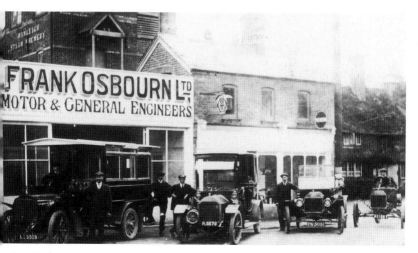

By 1934 business had expanded to the extent that Osbourn's moved to larger premises in front of The Brewery in the High Street where a complete range of hire vehicles for both large and small parties could be offered.

Before the First World War ex-army vehicles were in plentiful supply and David Manns had already acquired an impressive fleet of motorised and horse-drawn transport to support a wide range of services to customers. The driver of the Model T Ford is Mr Samuel Mann and the occupants of the motor cycle and side car are Mr & Mrs J.J. Mann

For centuries the horse and cart provided the most effective means of delivering goods or removal of house contents. Here David Mann's waggon is seen on its rounds, possibly in Shamley Green around 1908. The driver is W. Lynn but unfortunately the names of the boy and the dog are not recorded.

David Mann's claim to have introduced the first petrol-driven commercial vehicle into the village in 1913, and this cut the return journey time to London from two days to a morning. This picture shows a later version at the rear of the shop by the entrance to Victoria road.

By the 1920s motor transport had grown in popularity to the extent that Surrey villages such as Cranleigh became accessible to a much larger population. The Railway Hotel on The Common obviously provided a convenient stopping-off point for tea before the return journey to suburbia. The Hotel is also offering garage facilities and the volume of traffic is such as to require the services of the village "bobby".

The Aldershot & District autobus awaits passengers at Cranleigh station before departing for Plaistow. Other omnibus services in the village were offered by Tillingbourne, Gastonia, and Pioneer.

This scene from the 1940s shows the bicycle as the predominant form of transport with just the occasional appearance of the motor car.

By the late fifties a wide range of motor transport was available to even the average family. As a result, parking is now becoming a major problem.

Four

Village Life

In Edwardian times fox hunting was a popular pastime in the village. The Meet often took place near the Obelisk and Dr Napper can be seen in the middle of the three men standing on the left.

For over 160 years the Onslow Arms has been a Public House in the centre of the village, providing a meeting place for refreshment and recreation. Named after the famous family previously resident in Knowle House and now living at Clandon, the hotel offered rooms for letting, stabling for six horses, a coach house and carriages to and from the station.

The Greyhound Inn was said to be a run-down property in the last century but improvements resulted in a white stucco-fronted building complete with a porch supported by classical pillars. Extensions provided for a club room, public rooms, a brewhouse, coach house and stables. At this time it is decorated in celebration of the 1935 Jubilee.

Before it closed in 1937 the Greyhound enjoyed over 100 years of successful trade. Fairs and similar celebrations were held in the field to the rear of the building and during the war a room was used by the Civil Defence to demonstrate anti-gas precautions. It remained derelict until it was demolished to make way for the present Post Office.

Originally built as a private dwelling the Boy and Donkey became a public house in the last century. When this picture was taken the licensee was Mr Sydney Collins. In more recent times it was the scene of re-enactment of Civil War battles. Sadly the pub has just recently reverted to a private house once again.

Cranley Hotel, 1930s. The old Railway Hotel previously occupied the adjacent timber-clad building known as Laundry Cottage. Early this century it transferred to the present red-brick building complete with ornamental 'Dutch' gables. The name was changed to the more acceptable Cranley Hotel in 1929 just before this picture was taken.

The Glories of Empire were calls for annual celebration on Queen Victoria's birthday 24 May. Clearly an important occasion for socialising amidst speech-making and saluting the Union Jack.

At first sight this appears to be the same event as the picture above but from the inscription on the reverse it is one year later. Note the additional growth of the Magnolia trees against the Lady Peek building.

A meeting of the Chiddingfold Hunt near the cricket field on the common taken from Wellers' building on the corner of Rowland road. The old bank building can be seen outside the station, and the large shed behind was used for unloading. Weller store and hoist to the grain loft can be seen in the distance.

After the First World War events were held on the Common to raise funds for war widows and orphans. The organiser on this occasion is the Old Pals' Club and the Cranleigh Brass and Reed Band are providing the musical entertainment.

Scouting has remained a popular activity in the village for the last 90 or so years. The Cranleigh troop met in the old Baptist chapel in Chapel Place and field range exercises were held on Smithwood Common and in wartime against the Local Defence Corps.

Cranleigh's Brass and Reed Band, affectionately known as the 'spit and dribble,' is pictured in 1913 on the occasion of the Southern Counties Challenge Cup competition. Promenade Concerts were given frequently in the summer at various parts of the village and common under their Conductor, Mr J. Blacklidge.

Lych Gate & Institute, Cranleigh.

Nightingale
Ewhurst Rd. Series
W.H.A. 2861.

Built by Sir Henry Peek in 1985 in memory of his wife, the Lady Peek Institute was a Mens' Club offering a bar, rooms for billiards, cards and reading together with bedrooms for the use of its members. Since its closure the building has housed the Library, Citizens Advice Bureau and more recently offices.

The Cricket Green, Cranleigh.

Delves, Stationer
Cranleigh

The Cricket field has provided a focus for sporting activities since 1843 and is one of the oldest greens in Surrey. Apart from many famous cricketers who have played on the turf, Peter May was a well known resident until his recent death. Another famous village resident was Frank Swinnerton, the celebrated author, who lived in the large house on the other side of the field.

After the Second World War the thatched roof of the old wooden building caught fire and was replaced by a new brick and tile construction.

The victorious tug-o-war team outside the Greyhound Inn just before the Second World War. It is said that most, if not all, were members of the Buckman family, many of whom later served in the Local Defence Volunteers.

'A Midsummer Night's Dream' performed by the boys at the National School in 1922. It was not seemly for the girls to take part in mixed entertainment and in true pantomime fashion the boys borrowed dresses in order to play the female parts.

Harry Buckman is seen here outside his cobbler's shop on the Common. His son Stan later became the projectionist and manager in the local picture house which residents will remember as the old Co-op shop. When the lease was not renewed Stan set about gaining support from local businessmen to build a new cinema on land previously occupied by his father's shop.

The Regal Cinema was eventually opened in October 1936 by Lady Bonham, when the film being shown was Walter Huston in 'Rhodes of Africa'. Said at the time to resemble a miniature Gaumont, it orignally seated 466 people but this was recently reduced to a more comfortable 266. The present owners have kept pace with the latest developments and Cranleigh is one of the last places of comparable size to retain its original cinema.

Five

The Village at Work

Cheesmans carriage works and paint shop was in the building now known as Little Causey. The hot steel bands were shrunk on to wooden wheels, the cooling process giving rise to huge clouds of steam. The finished carriages were winched up into the upper shop for painting by Jim Laker in a dust-free atmosphere. All this activity provided much free entertainment for pupils on their way home from school.

George Bruford opened his Steam Brewery in 1876 and by the end of the century was able to offer a wide range of beers, spirits, and mineral waters. The Three Horseshoes public house had been in existence long before the brewery and owed its name to its proximity to one of the three smithies.

Brewing would have created its own atmosphere and the smell of hops would have been all pervasive. The most common footwear for the workers was wooden clogs and this, together with the sound of horseshoes on cobbles, would have produced a sound of great industry.

Telephone—15, P.O.

BRUFORD & Co., Ltd.,
CRANLEIGH BREWERY.

ALE AND STOUT.

BREWED FROM THE BEST MALT AND HOPS.

List of Prices.

In Cask..	4½-gal.		9-gal.		18-gal.		36-gal.	
	s.	d.	s.	d.	s.	d.	s.	d.
XXXX	7	6	15	0	30	0	60	0
XXX Pale Ale ..	6	0	12	0	24	0	48	0
XX Pale Ale ...	4	6	9	6	18	0	36	0
X Pale Ale ...	3	9	7	6	15	0	30	0
I.P.A. India Pale Ale	5	3	10	6	21	0	42	0
B.B. Bitter Beer	4	6	9	0	18	0	36	0
S.A. Harvest Ale	—		6	0	12	0	24	0
(Not less than 9 galls. supplied.)								
Double Stout ...	7	6	15	0	30	0	60	0
Single Stout ...	6	0	12	0	24	0	48	0
Porter ...	4	6	9	0	18	0	36	0
Disct. for Cash on Delivery	3d.		6d.		1/-		2/-	

BOTTLED BEERS.

O.E. Ale	...	...	...	Pints 3/6 per doz.
Dinner Ale	...	...	...	,, 2/6 ,, ,,
Pale Ale ...	...	½-pints 1/6	...	,, 3/- ,, ,,
Double Stout	...	...	...	,, 3/6 ,, ,,
Single Stout	...	..	...	,, 2/6 ,, ,,

In 4-Quart Crates.

Mild Ale	...	1/2	Single Stout 1/2 and 1/4
Bitter Ale	...	1/4	Double Stout ... 1/6

Guiness's Stout and Bass's Ale always in Stock.

The above advertisement from a directory of 1911 shows an extensive range of beers at prices quite clearly from another age.

Postmen waiting to begin their delivery rounds from outside the Post Office when it formed part of Rowlands Stores. The man on the left is Johnny Clayton, a well known character in the village and supporter of the football team for many years.

Opposite: The page from the local Almanac shows the extent of postal services available in 1911. Deliveries made three times a day and once on Sundays were quite considerable for such a small community.

LOCAL POSTAL REGULATIONS.

POST OFFICE—*Corner Knowle Lane.*
Postmaster—*Mr. L. C. Burdett.*

DELIVERIES—Weekdays : 6.35 a.m. 12.10, 5.45 p.m. *Sundays* 7.0 a.m.

DESPATCHES—Weekdays : 10.30 a.m., 1.10, 3.40, 5.45, and 7.50 p.m. *Sundays* 10.50 a.m.

PARCEL POST DESPATCHES—Week-days only : 10.20 a.m., 1.0, 3.30, 5.35, 6.30, and 7.50 p.m.

TELEGRAMS—Week-days from 8.0 a.m. till 8.0 p.m. *Sundays* 8.30 till 10.0 a.m.

TELEPHONE—Continuous Service.

GENERAL BUSINESS—Money Order and Savings' Bank Business (including Insurance and Annuity) from 8.0 a.m. till 8.0 p.m. on Week-days. Postal Orders are issued and paid from 8.0 a.m. till 8.0 p.m. on Week-days. General Business on Week-days from 8.0 a.m. till 8.0 p.m. and on Sundays from 8.30 till 10.0 a.m.

Time of clearing Letter Boxes.

	WEEKDAYS.			SUNDAYS.
	a.m.	p.m.	p.m.	a.m.
Station	10.20	1.0	6.15	... 11.0
The Common	9.20	12.30	5.50	... 11.5
The Brewery	10.20	1.0	6.30 7.40	... 9.50
Guildford Road... ...	9.10	12.40	6.0	... 9.35
Ewhurst Road	9.20	12.30	6.20	.. 9.45
Nanhurst	7.10	1.30	6.0	... 8.0
Hall Place	7.40	1.0	5.50	... 8.30
Elm Bridge Road ...	8.25	2.0	6.5	... 9.15
Withybush	7.35	1.10	6.25	... 8.0
Bookers Lea	8.20	1.40	4.45	... 8.45
Gaston Gate	8.25	6.0	--	... 11.15
Alderbrook	7.25	2.15	6.0	... 11.10
Snoxhall	7.5	12.35	6.30	... 7.30
Winterfold	8.40	1.15	5.50	... 9.20
Horsham Road	9.0	1.30	6.15	... 8.40

The Windmill on the Common stood for over 100 years before it was dismantled in 1917. The octagonal tower of the smock pattern is clearly seen in this picture although this structure itself replaced a much older post mill.

The Killick family operated the mill for most of the last century until 1880 when the Weller Brothers took it over. Thomas, William and Henry Killick were all involved at different times. When a length of sail broke off a gas engine was installed, supplied from the nearby works.

The Weller Brothers lorry is seen here making a delivery of corn to the mill. In February, 1917, after several attempts at preservation, the mill was dismantled by Jabez Nightingale and the timbers used by a Mr Davis who restored several old houses in Cranleigh. A resident returning from fighting in France told of his distress in rounding the corner of the Guildford Road to find the windmill had gone for ever. Weller Brothers had erected several ancillary buildings around the mill in the decades around the turn of the century and these are all that now remain.

The Gasworks on the Common owned by Stephen Rowland were built on the site of the old workhouse. The Cranleigh Gas Company opened in 1876 and had its own railway sidings where coal was unloaded. It closed soon after nationalisation of the gas industry in 1948.

The gas holder stood until it was hit by a flying bomb in 1944. Mrs Ede, who lived in the nearby cottage, was killed by the blast. Now only the brick wall remains to remind us of the old workhouse.

The old family firm of Holden's was world famous for the use of old seasoned oak in the making of bell frames. The timber was cut on steam powered saws fuelled with off-cuts. Unfortunately, possibly as a result of a spark, a disastrous fire occurred in 1906 which destroyed most of the works and sadly many of the workers' personal tools.

Cranleigh, Windmill Road

Above: Before the advent of motorised transport, grass on the cricket field was cut by a horse-drawn mower. To prevent the hoofs damaging the turf leather over-shoes were strapped on to each foot.

Left: At the turn of the century much of the employment was based on agriculture. The well known character in the picture is Ned Stedman, a labourer employed at Stonewall, a large farm which owned much of the land behind the houses on the north side of the High Street.

Six

The War Years

In the First World War Mrs E. Rowcliffe of Hall Place ran a nursing home at Oaklands in Knowle Lane for wounded soldiers. Seen here are some of the nurses with a group of walking wounded. The building has now been pulled down to make room for a modern residence.

During the First World War Cranleigh was home to the Oxfordshire and Buckinghamshire Light Infantry who were billetted in various houses around the village. This picture is taken from the postcard sent in 1916 and the sender has identified himself with a cross. Who can guess what fate awaits them and how many of them ever returned?

Mr Jesse Mann with his wife and her younger sisters photographed with four soldiers from the Ox and Bucks Light Infantry. In the Second World War, whilst living in Oliver House, soldiers were offered the facility to bath in his house for the payment of a small fee.

Above: A group of 'walking wounded' from "Oaklands" recuperating on Cranleigh Common. This postcard was issued in memory of those who died, and exhorts the patients to make a rapid recovery with the epithet "Cheer up, my Brothers, Go yet once again, Drive the veiled monster, Back into his den."

Right: One fine young son of a Cranleigh family was Private Jack Charles of the Suffolk Regiment who died in Flanders aged 20. Jack was the eldest child of a family of five children, all of whom were born in the village and have enjoyed a close association with the various aspects of Cranleigh life for over a century.

Cranleigh's War Memorial was unveiled and dedicated by the Rector, Rev. Philip Cunningham, in December 1920. Today the Memorial still shows where one name has been erased. One returning soldier called Stedman was surprised to see his brother's name amongst those listed and reported to the authorities that he was alive and well and sitting at home.

In May 1940 when invasion seemed imminent Cranleigh immediately formed a band of Local Defence Volunteers and so the local 'Dad's Army' began! Five observation posts were set up at New Park, Holdhurst, Rowley Farm, Smithwood Common and Bookhurst Hill. Exercises in Baynards Park used bicycles as the principle means of transport. Cranleigh's 'E' Company of the Home Guard was made up of many old family names such as Buckman, Moyer, Pullen, Mann, Killick, Cheesman, Eede, Tickner, and Napper.

Women also had a role to play as auxiliaries in the Signal Section. This section under the command of Lieut. Miles enlisted and trained women for static signal duties and it is reported 'that they soon mastered the intricate army line and wireless procedures.'

In June 1943 the Home Guard co-operated in the defence of Dunsfold aerodrome. A contemporary report recalls memories of the days at Parkhatch during the summer. 'These were strenuous Sundays with excellent hot meals provided under the oak trees by our own company cooks from their self-made field kitchen. Cpl. Abbot and his cooks gave us hot tea and a two-course meal for dinner – good days good food!'

May, 1944, was the occasion of 'Salute the Soldier' week when the salute was taken by Field-Marshal Lord Milne. RSM Gamble is credited with skillfully handling a large number of assorted units and services who assembled on the common before marching through the High Street. Here a platoon of WRACs gives the salute outside the station; the Old Bank House can be clearly seen in the background.

Opposite above: A detachment of the RAF standing to attention outside Bank Buildings. Lieut-Colonel Hopewell can be seen in the inspection party as commanding officer of the Home Guard. Bearing more than a passing resemblance to Captain Mainwaring, he was a master at Cranleigh School but managed to combine both duties throughout the war.

Opposite below: The ladies take their turn again. No doubt many will still be able to recognise themselves or relatives in this picture.

In 1944 a 'flying bomb' hit the Junior School behind St Nicholas Church destroying the east window and nearly demolishing the school. Fortunately this was on a Sunday morning when the school was empty, otherwise fatalities would have occurred. Another direct hit on Cranleigh was on the gasholder on the Common, destroying it and a nearby cottage, killing the occupant.

Seven

Three Villages

SHAMLEY GREEN.

Going north from Cranleigh the traveller will pass through the village of Shamley Green.
Overlooking the cricket green is the Red Lion public house, which dates from the 17th century.
The adjoining cottages and the nearby old forge make an attractive group of buildings.

Shamley Green.

No. 2.

Shamley Green (once known as Shamble Lea) is a delightful village, charmingly laid out around two wide greens. Past and present inhabitants of the village include car builder W.O. Bentley, Alfred Hitchcock, T.S. Eliot and TV personality Tony Hart.

Shamley Green.

A view of the green showing the wagon of the carrier Mr J. Knight of Cranleigh, pausing for a break on its way back from Guildford. Whilst the horse appreciates his nosebag Mr Knight is no doubt taking liquid refreshment in the Red Lion!

Above: The village boasts many fine timber-framed houses but amongst the best of these is Barn Cottage with two fine chimneys, situated near the beginning of Woodhill Lane. The Post Office was housed here from 1890 until it moved across the green in 1930.

Right: This picture of the Gamekeeper at Willingshurst was taken by local Shamley Green photographer Mr Walter Sayers. Apart from taking many of the old photographs of the village Mr Sayers mended cycles, repaired shoes and sold sweets and tobaccos from a small shed at the bottom of Sweetwater Lane.

Wonersh, 1902, is recorded in earlier times as Wogenhersh, Ognersh, Woronish. In the fourteenth century Wonersh was famous for woad, the blue dye used in the manufacture of cloth, and several of the cottages in The Street were the homes of weavers. Seen here the local postman is about to begin his deliveries from the nearby post office.

At the centre of the village is the Grantley Arms. Built around 1600 it was formerly called the Hector Inn and later The George. It is named after Lord Grantley, MP for Guildford, and Speaker of the House of Commons, who lived in Wonersh Park until 1884. The timber-framed facade has been changed many times with the addition of stiffening braces.

The Grantley Arms, 1910. The brewer's dray is just making a delivery together with wines and spirits from the Guildford Stores. The facade has been modified from the earlier picture and now offers open and closed carriages for hire.

Wheelers Stores built in 1889 provides villagers with a wide range of supplies and groceries and the post office has moved to small premises on the side. Today the shop still provides general stores and Post Office for the village.

Wonersh Village.

The curiously shaped bus shelter nicknamed the "Pepper Pot" by villagers was designed and given to the village by architect R.H. Haslem in 1928. Bricks from the former Ice House at Wonersh Place were used for the base and, despite recent attempts by lorry drivers to demolish it, the villagers insist on retaining their unique landmark.

The Mill House, built c. 1550, is a four bay timber framed house built on the other side of the pond away from the mill itself. Despite later additions the house today retains much of its old world charm.

Entrance, St. John's Seminary, Wonersh.

St John's Seminary, built in 1891, under the direction of its founder bishop John Butt. When choosing the site it is said the bishop walked up the hill, paused for breath, placed his crozier in the ground and the spot was selected. It is a Roman Catholic college where men are trained to be secular priests.

St. John's Seminary, Wonersh.

Built on part of Lostiford Farm, haymaking was carried out and helping on the farm was part of the students' daily chores. It remained a working farm with pigs, cows and poultry until after the Second World War.

Bramley c. 1903. The Jolly Farmer public house, formerly called The Wheatsheaf, is housed in a fine 18th century building and was previously supplied by its own brewery until taken over by Bruford's Cranleigh Brewery in 1904.

Bramley Church of England Village school was opened in 1851. How different life must have been when this picture was taken with high incidence of absenteeism due to illness and violent storms rendering the roads in the outlying districts impassable. An entry for the log book of 1905 says the work during the week has been carried on under difficulties, the Master being responsible for the instruction of some 75 children in a room accommodating 60.

The Station.   Sincere smiles, P.C,   Bramley, Surrey.

This peaceful scene shows some of the station staff and passengers outside Bramley Station. There was a house provided for the Station Master, with adjacent office, waiting room and toilets. Sadly, today only the Post Office letter box remains.

Bramley Station.

The Horsham train is just arriving at Bramley and Wonersh Station, renamed in 1888. In 1942 a Guildford bound train full of Christmas shoppers was bombed and tragically seven people were killed, including the driver and the guard; many more were injured.

Bramley Mill is sighted in Mill Lane next to a picturesque pond, one of many along this tributary along the River Wey. It was first recorded in 1295 and may be even earlier than this. In his book *Highways & Byways in Surrey*, Eric Parker describes The Old Mill as ' ... the prettiest thing in Bramley, with its medlar tree overhanging the water, its ducks and pigeons, its octagonal brick dovecot and lichened roofs, and its sweet-water grape vine clambering on the old walls, has a rich grace of colour and age setting it, in modern Bramley, a thing apart.'

Eight

Towards Stane Street

Leaving Cranleigh and travelling east one soon encounters the small wealden village of Ewhurst, so named after the large number of yew trees growing in the area. Situated on the true wealden clay, the road from Ewhurst to Ockley was described by William Cobbett on one of his 'rural rides' as 'the deepest clay that I ever saw'. Today with its pond, church, green and views towards Coneyhurst Hill the village retains much of its old world charm.

The buildings around the church gate are now private houses but were once a grocer's shop and a public house which later became the Post Office.

Like most villages in the area, even the small ones, Ewhurst boasted its own blacksmith's forge. This is now the site of a car showroom next to The Bull's Head public house.

At the turn of the century a number of old buildings clustered around the village green providing a wide range of trades for the local people. A delivery of besom brooms is just being made to the village stores which also houses the post office. Next door H. Goldman offers a range of horse-drawn and motor carriages. Before the Bull's Head was built on the opposite side of the road the village local was The Crown Inn, supplied by Brewers Lascelles & Tickner of Guildford.

In this later view, taken from behind the buildings around the village green, the Bull's Head can be seen in the background.

The present building replaces this earlier one burnt down in 1906 and commands spectacular views over The Weald, towards the South Downs. The location was said to be a favourite haunt of smugglers, making their way northwards with their contraband and shaking off the pursuers amongst the wild tracks of the Hurtwood.

On the summit of Winterfold hill stands the windmill, now a private dwelling almost completely obscured by surrounding trees. The present tower dates from 1845 when the previous post mill blew down in a storm. In an account of 1838, local schoolboy John Elliot reports "I do not think all Windmills are made alike, some are built upon posts like that one at Ewhurst which I saw one day when we went for a walk". In Georgian times the mill would have provided a prominent landmark on the horizon for smugglers finding their way to London.

Under Holmbury Hill lies the small village of Forest Green. Overlooking the green is the Parrot Inn, a favourite watering hole of smugglers in former times and tourists today. Originally a small private dwelling dating from the 17th century, the present premises have been enlarged to provide facilities for a considerable local and passing trade.

Forest Green, aptly named, the hamlet is seen as a green clearing in the forest when viewed from nearby Leith Hill. The church was built in 1892 by the Hensley family as a memorial to their son Everard, tragically killed in a shooting accident.

Today Forest Green has no shops but in times when commuting was more difficult supplies were available locally at A.H. Jays. The premises shown in this picture have long since been converted into private dwellings.

After Jays left the village to set up in Shere the stores passed to Stringers who also ran the post office. From these modest premises it seems they were able to offer groceries, bread, boots and shoes and gents' clothing.

Nine

The Fold Country

Alfold Crossways in 1910 still retained a road layout emanating from the old turnpike system. The boy is standing in the Alfold road and the route to the left goes towards Dunsfold. The bypass has yet to be constructed and the Horsham road can still be seen as a branch from the main route. The building just visible on the left is the orginal tollhouse which dates from around 1760.

In Edwardian times Alfold was typical of most villages in being centred around the essential church, shop, and public house. The double-fronted Randall's Stores has now reverted to a private house but the Crown Inn retains much of its character marked by the unusual arched window.

This scene typifies village life in Edwardian times. The appearance of the camera intrigues the two little girls outside the shop, whilst the brewer's drey is just making a delivery to the Crown. The road through the village is part of the Guildford to Arundel turnpike and was completed in 1809.

Mr Randall watches from his shop doorway whilst the wagon is being loaded. The entrance to the church is between the charming tile-hung cottages, and the churchyard on the left. Much of the earlier prosperity of the region derives from glass-making, and amongst the ancient gravemarkers is one to Hugenot Jean Carre who died in 1572.

Part of the church of St Nicholas is Norman and the bell turret dates from the 15th century. The stocks can be seen near the entrance, protected by a small roofed structure.

Alfold elementary schools was erected in 1876. The village was fortunate in possessing such an impressive facility with a population of only 600 when this picture was taken, and these pupils certainly look happy with their lot. No doubt people still living in the village will be able to recognise themselves or their playmates from this picture. Recently the school was closed by the local authority and is now a private school for 3–5 year olds.

ALFOLD HOUSE.

Maximum advantage of the proximity of the great Wealden forest is taken in the many timbered framed houses and cottages in the village. Alfold House is the most picturesque and its 16th century period shows a construction at the transition between close and widely spaced timbering.

Despite the main thoroughfare and the proximity of the canal Alfold has retained much of its small village atmosphere. The Alford Village Stores continues to provide groceries and provisions for the village. The small castellated building on the right housed the Post Office for many years.

Park Hatch Lodge, Dunsfold, 1906. Present day inhabitants will have no trouble recognising this location opposite the turning to Dunsfold. The house and wall remains today much as it was ninety years ago when this picture was taken by Cranleigh photographer H.U. Knight.

Park Hatch was by all accounts a grand house set on the southern slopes of Hascombe Hill in a deer park of about 200 acres. It was the seat of Mr Joseph Godman and the grounds were put to good use for exercises in the Second World War. The picture shows a meet of the local Chiddingfold hounds.

Dunsfold's thirteenth-century church lies some half a mile from the village centre. A complete church of the period is something of a rarity and its fine stained glass gives an unusually light and airy appearance. The wooden bench pews also date from this period and are thought to be the oldest surviving in Britain.

Unlike Alfold, Dunsfold's disposition around its large common has been described variously as 'scattered', 'open' and more unkindly as 'straggling'. There is no doubt that in former times the large expanse of grass was put to maximum use by animals and inhabitants alike.

DUNSFOLD.

When this picture of the Common was taken the Alfold Road was barely wide enough for cars to pass. The old pollarded trees were in the process of being removed and the Sun public House can be seen in the background.

Dunsfold Mill, 1906. Today little remains to remind us of the impressive water mill which once stood near to the present dwelling known as Mill House. The site lies on a tributary of the River Arun and near to the Roman road which can be traced from Chiddingfold.

Ten

South into Sussex

Travelling south from Cranleigh, passing the entrances to Baynards Park and Pollingfold Manor, the traveller soon enters the hamlet of Ellens Green. The impressive but not so old Ellens is a relatively modern expansion of the much older Ellens Farm which dates from Tudor times and was still a working farm when this picture was taken. The large building has now been divided into three separate dwellings.

Rudgwick Street.

About 5 miles south lies Rudgwick and, although over the border in Sussex, it has been naturally linked to Cranleigh by the turnpike road since the early eighteen hundreds. A number of splendid tile-hung houses are typified by this row of cottages.

This view, which is one of a series known as 'Rural England', was taken by a local Slinfold photographer. The name Rudgwick, or Rudgewick as it was spelt, is derived from the Old English meaning the place on the ridge, and the village's position on a sandstone ridge can be clearly seen.

Eames Cottage, 1910. Built around 1600, this charming house is a superb example of a tile hung residence of the period with a Horsham slab roof typical of this local area. At the time the picture was taken the house was occupied by the family of Mr W.H. 'Billy' Butcher. He was also the local butcher operating from the premises next door, and by all accounts was a great character responsible for organising many events in the village.

In 1920 the Post Office was under the control of Mr Moses Humphrey who also provided groceries and drapery. In the pony cart Mr Dewdeney the baker is just making his delivery round. The high front entrance was clearly designed to facilitate mounting a horse and the box provided a convenient receptacle for unloading a cart.

When the village stores closed and the building reverted to a private dwelling the Post Office moved across the road to Woes cottage and is now housed in a separate building in the garden.

The King's Head is said to have been named after George IV, for whom this was a favourite watering place on his trips between Windsor and Brighton. The buildings have grown over the years and now obstruct the view of the church from the road although they are probably built over dwellings used by the masons working on the tower in the 14th century.

The large house which was once the old Sanitorium in Rudgwick can still be recognised from its curious shaped chimney. Earlier this century TB was a common and often fatal disease for which there was no satisfactory cure. The recommended treatment was fresh air at all times regardless of temperature, which accounts for the wide open windows and doors.

Rudgwick Station, 1912. When the railway between Horsham and Guildford opened in 1865 Rudgwick was excluded from the celebrations. The Inspecting Officer adjudged the gradient in the station to be too steep for safety and required the embankment to be raised, and a further level to be added to the Arun bridge.

Seen from the bridge, the extent of the sidings becomes apparent. Goods traffic was mainly coal and agricultural products although the volume moved never matched expectations. Soon after the line closed in 1965 the platform and buildings were demolished to make way for a health centre.

The Martlet Hotel, in 1912, was an impressive ivy-clad building capable of accommodating a large number of visitors. At one time the white gates could be closed to keep out unwanted intruders and locals would often drop into the Martlet rather than face the climb up to the King's Head. Sadly the rush of visitors never materialised and the site is now occupied by a parade of modern shops.

The Queen's Head Hotel, 1910, on the main road between Guildford and Horsham was a favourite coaching stop in the last century. The blacksmith's forge was conveniently situated opposite and the horse could be left in the shade of the tree which is sadly no more. The steam-powered dray is making a delivery from the Rock Brewery, and King & Chasemore's hoarding advertises several desirable properties.

Bibliography

Alderman, H.M.: *The Charm of Old Surrey*, 1935
Collison-Morley, L.: *Companion into Surrey*, 1938
Cracknell, Basil E.: *Portrait of Surrey*, 1970
English, Judie: *Cranleigh–a historical walk*, 1985
Hope Moncrieff, A.R.: *Surrey painted by Sutton Palmer*, 1906
Hodd, H.R.: *The Horsham–Guildford Direct Railway*, 1975
Howkins, Christopher: *Hidden Surrey*, 1987
Lambert, F.A.H.: *Surrey–The Little Guides*, 1903
Mann, S.: *Cranley in ye Olden Days & Cranleigh Today*
Maxwell, Donald: *Unknown Surrey*, 1924
Mee, Arthur: *Surrey The King's England*, 1938
Mitchell, V., and Smith, K.: *Branch Lines to Horsham*, 1982
Parker, Eric: *Highways and Byways in Surrey*, 1908
Parker, Eric: *Surrey The County Books*, 1947
Seymour, B., and Warrington, M.: *Bygone Cranleigh*, 1984
Turner, Dennis: *Surrey Ordnance Survey Historical Guides*, 1988
Vine, P.A.L.: *London's Lost Route to the Sea*, 1986
Viney, Gwen: *Memories of Cranleigh*, 1992
Walker, Peggy: *Rudgwick Memories*, 1993

Acknowledgements

In writing this book I am aware of many friends who have given me help and encouragement since my family moved to this charming part of Surrey. They have always given generously of their time and loaned their treasured personal pictures for copying and inclusion in this book. In particular I would like to thank Nigel Balchin, Robin Brand, Frank and Muriel Charles, Ivor Charles, Roy Collins, Terry Disley, Major D.C. Elliot, Judie English, Roy Foster, N. Hamshere, Dick House, Gillian Whitelaw, W. Stone and the Francis Frith Collection. Special appreciation is also due to John Janaway and the staff of Surrey Local Studies Library, Harvey Ide of the Cranleigh Camera Shop for so expertly copying quantities of original material, and Bernard and Pat Tonks of the Regal Cinema.